D0272880

Penguin
Random
House

Senior Editor Tori Kosara
Project Editor Lisa Stock
Editor Anant Sagar
Art Editor Pallavi Kapur
DTP Designer Umesh Singh Rawat
Pre-production Producer Siu Yin Chan
Pre-production Manager Sunil Sharma
Senior Producer Alex Bell
Managing Editors Sadie Smith, Chitra Subramanyam
Managing Art Editors Neha Ahuja, Ron Stobbart
Publisher Julie Ferris
Art Director Lisa Lanzarini
Publishing Director Simon Beecroft

Designed for DK by Mark Richards

For Lucasfilm
Executive Editor Jonathan W. Rinzler
Art Director Troy Alders
Story Group Rayne Roberts, Pablo Hidalgo, Leland Chee

Reading Consultant Maureen Fernandes

First published in Great Britain in 2015 by
Dorling Kindersley Limited
80 Strand, London, WC2R 0RL
A Penguin Random House Company

10 9 8 7 6 5 4 3
003–275293–July/2015

A CIP catalogue record for this book is available from the British Library.

ISBN: 978-0-24118-634-3

Printed in China

Contents

The story of Darth Vader

Take a look at Darth Vader – if you dare! He is a very dangerous man with many terrifying powers. Darth Vader is a ruthless Sith Lord who helps rule the galaxy for the evil Emperor Palpatine.

But Darth Vader was not always the masked Sith you see now. Once he was a talented Jedi Knight named Anakin Skywalker. Read on and uncover the story of how a promising young Jedi turned to the dark side of the Force.

TWO SIDES OF
THE FORCE

The Force is an invisible energy that flows through all living things. Force sensitive beings can learn to control its power. But they must also choose which side to follow.

THE DARK SIDE

The Sith follow the dark side of the Force, which feeds on negative feelings such as anger and fear. They use the dark side to gain unlimited power and dangerous knowledge.

DARK SIDE TRAITS

- DOMINANCE
- GREED
- TERRIFYING POWER
- AMBITION
- PASSION

THE LIGHT SIDE

The Jedi follow the light side of the Force. They use it to protect the innocent and fight for justice. The light side of the Force guides Jedi to act honestly and with compassion. It also allows them to live in harmony with the beings and nature of the galaxy.

LIGHT SIDE TRAITS

BRAVERY

PEACE

INNER STRENGTH

JUSTICE

WISDOM

WHICH SIDE WOULD YOU CHOOSE?

Young Anakin Skywalker

Anakin Skywalker grew up a slave on the desert planet Tatooine. His mother Shmi could not explain how Anakin came to be born – he had no father.

Anakin was a gentle child and he loved his mother very much. From a young age he was skilled at making and fixing mechanical things. When he was nine years old he built a droid called C-3PO to help his mother. However, Anakin was impulsive and liked to take risks.

A special calling

When Jedi Qui-Gon Jinn and
Obi-Wan Kenobi landed on Tatooine
to repair their ship, they met Anakin
Skywalker. Qui-Gon realised Anakin
had the potential to be a great Jedi.
Anakin offered to enter a dangerous
Podrace for Qui-Gon.

The Jedi Knight seized the opportunity
to win the parts he needed for his ship
and Anakin's freedom. He was sure that
Anakin's Force powers would help him
to win the race. He was right. Freed
from slavery, Anakin was able to leave
Tatooine with the Jedi, but first he had
to say goodbye to his mother.

A new life begins

After leaving Tatooine, Qui-Gon asked the Jedi Council to let Anakin become his apprentice, but it refused. The Council thought that Anakin was already too old, and some wise members also sensed danger in Anakin's future.

Anakin and the Jedi liberated the planet Naboo from the Trade Federation invasion. When Anakin destroyed the Trade Federation's Droid Control Ship, the Jedi Council changed its mind. Although Qui-Gon had been killed by a Sith, Obi-Wan promised to train Anakin instead.

Meet Queen Amidala

The young queen of Naboo is a very popular leader. Not only is she brave and loyal, she is also an expert with a blaster!

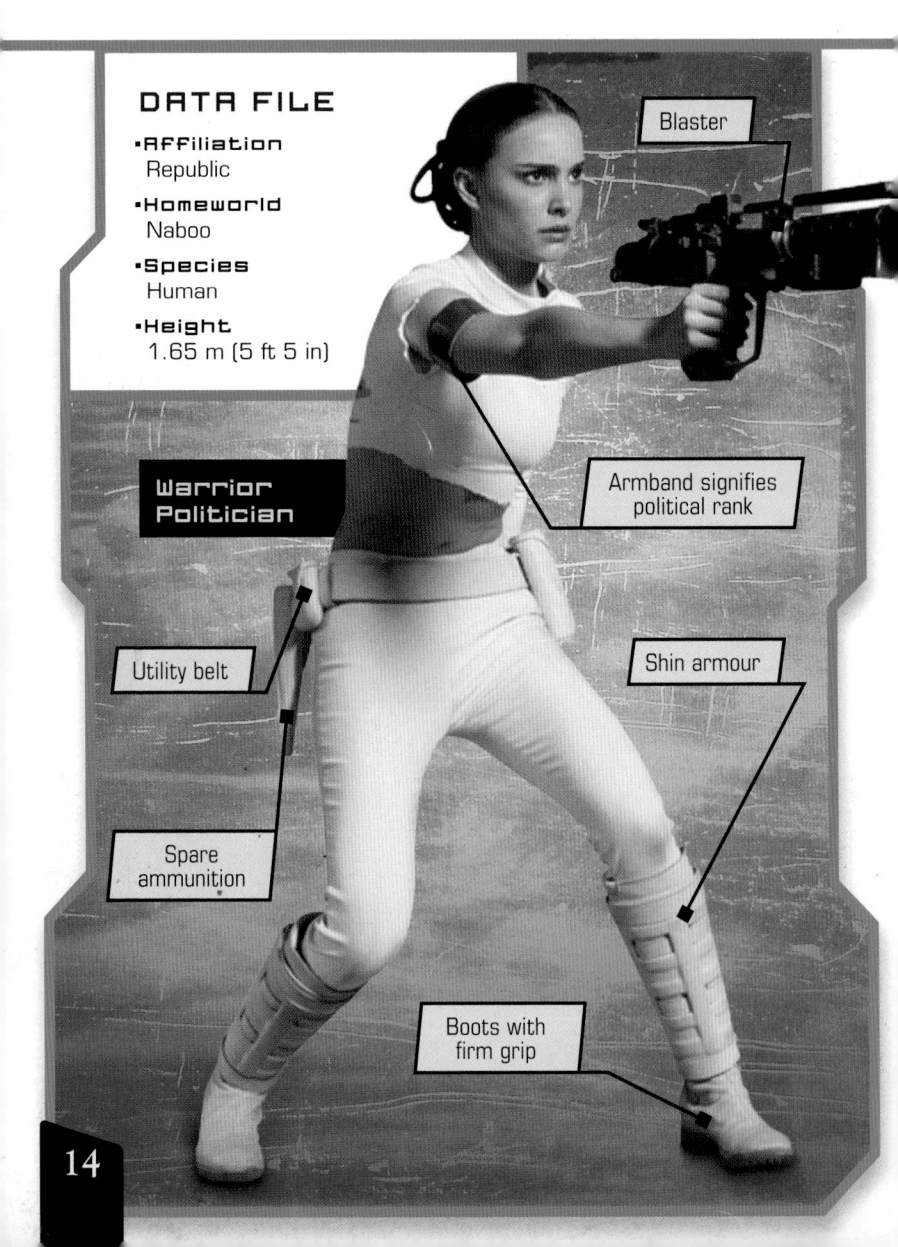

DATA FILE

- **Affiliation**
  Republic
- **Homeworld**
  Naboo
- **Species**
  Human
- **Height**
  1.65 m (5 ft 5 in)

Warrior Politician

Blaster

Armband signifies political rank

Utility belt

Shin armour

Spare ammunition

Boots with firm grip

Royal jewel of Zenda

Regal Ruler

Gold faceframes

Hem made from potolli fur

Intricate gold embroidery

Glowing Sein jewel

Jedi training

Anakin Skywalker returned to the Jedi Temple on the capital planet Coruscant to begin his training. He was taught how to use and control his incredible Force powers. Anakin was also instructed in the ways of the Jedi Knights. Jedi must not be governed by emotions. They are peace-loving, calm and use their skills only to defend, never to attack.

As Jedi Master Obi-Wan Kenobi's Padawan learner or apprentice, Anakin came to view Obi-Wan as the closest thing he had to a father figure.

Increasing frustration

Anakin loved and respected Obi-Wan, but often felt frustrated by him. Anakin was confident in his Jedi abilities, and felt that Obi-Wan was holding him back. He was tired of being just a Padawan.

Obi-Wan knew that Anakin had the potential to be a powerful Jedi Knight.

But he also believed that Anakin
had not yet mastered his emotions,
as a Jedi should. Obi-Wan was proved
right when Anakin was reunited with
Padmé Amidala after ten years.
The feelings that Anakin had felt
for her as a boy had not gone away.
Soon he would no longer be able
to control them.

Powerful friend

The galaxy was formed as a Republic, which meant that it was ruled by a Senate in which all the planets had representatives. As his frustration grew, Anakin found himself turning to Chancellor Palpatine, leader of the Republic.

Palpatine seemed to understand how Anakin felt. He was a good listener. Anakin believed that Palpatine was on his side, unlike Obi-Wan. Anakin did not realise that Palpatine was trying to destroy the Republic and seize power for himself.

Unstoppable feelings

Palpatine's sinister influence increased Anakin's frustration with Obi-Wan and the Jedi Order. He was feeling very confused. When he was chosen to escort Padmé back to Naboo, he finally lost the battle to control his feelings for her.

Padmé was now a Senator and had a duty to the Republic, but she too could not prevent herself from falling in love with Anakin. They were secretly married on Naboo. Jedi were not supposed to get emotionally attached to others. Anakin had broken the rules, but he didn't care.

Turning to the dark side

Anakin had not forgotten his mother Shmi, whom he had left on Tatooine. He began to have terrible nightmares about her, so he went to find her.

Anakin went back to Tatooine. There he discovered that Shmi had married a farmer named Cliegg Lars, who had freed her from slavery.

Anakin also learned that his mother had been kidnapped by Sand People. He went in search of her but he was too late and she died in his arms. Overcome with grief and anger, Anakin took revenge on the Sand People.

Jedi heroes

Although he was increasingly ruled by his emotions, Anakin had not yet fully turned to the dark side. When the Republic was forced into the Clone Wars, Anakin fought bravely with the Jedi.

The Clone Wars lasted for many years and Anakin and Obi-Wan became famous heroes.

Anakin felt truly alive in the heat of the battle and his powers became even stronger. However, Anakin still felt that he was being held back by the Jedi and that only Palpatine was encouraging his talents. He felt that maybe the Jedi teachings were not right and that greater power lay elsewhere.

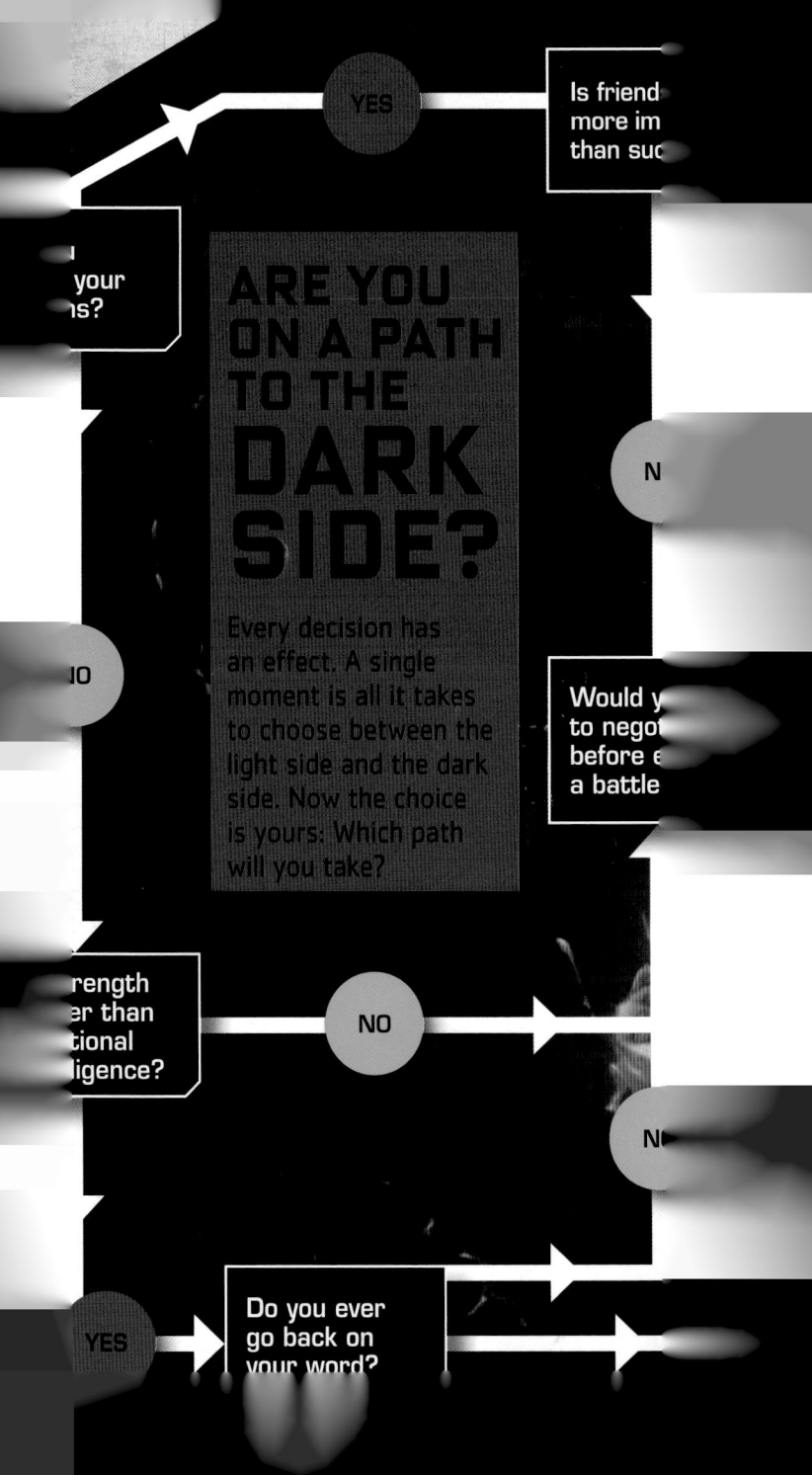

YES

Is friend[...]
more im[...]
than suc[...]

[...] your
[...]s?

ARE YOU
ON A PATH
TO THE
DARK
SIDE?

Every decision has
an effect. A single
moment is all it takes
to choose between the
light side and the dark
side. Now the choice
is yours: Which path
will you take?

N

Would y[...]
to nego[...]
before [...]
a battle

NO

[...]rength
[...]er than
[...]tional
[...]igence?

NO

N[...]

Do you ever
go back on
your word?

YES

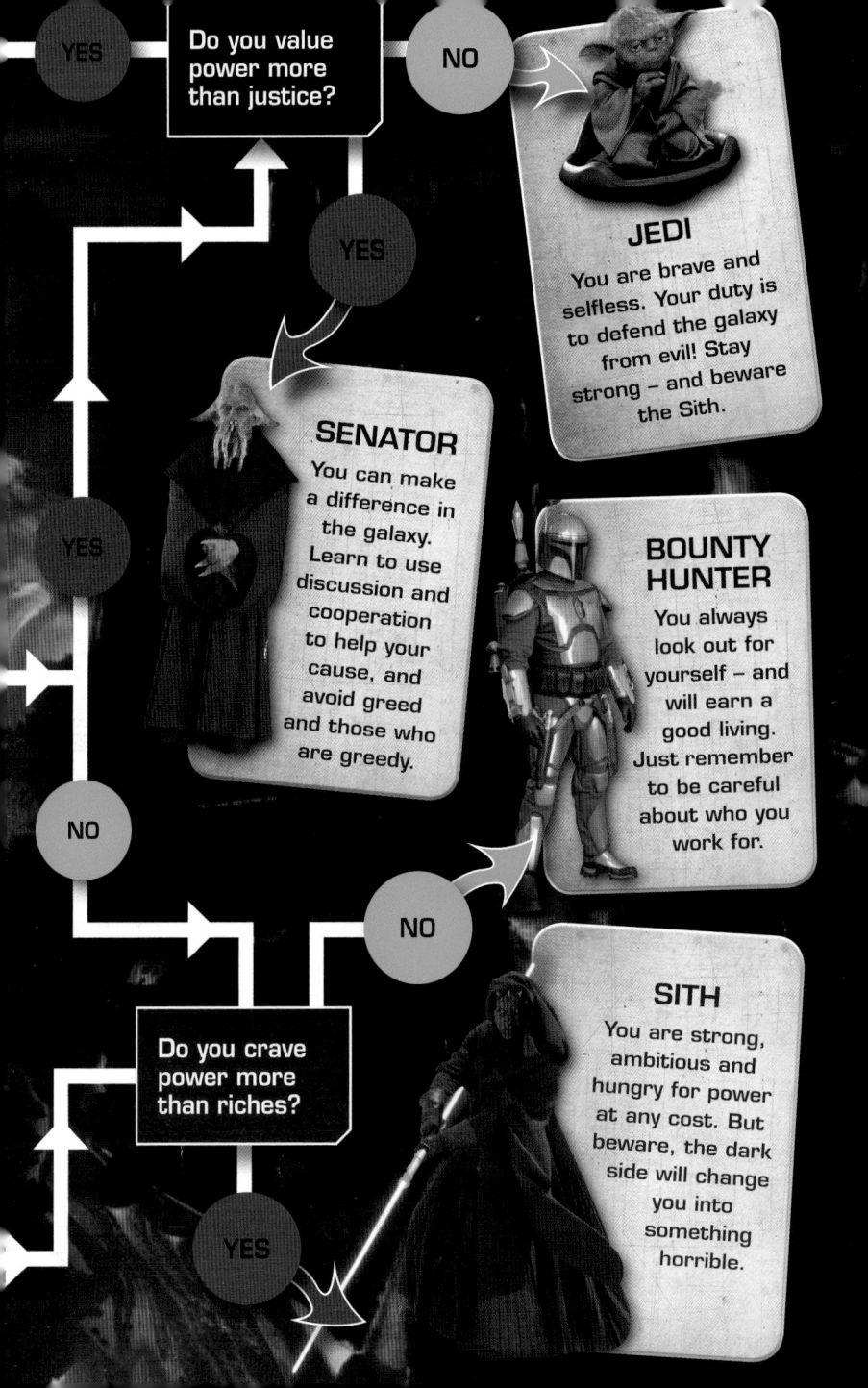

YES

Do you value power more than justice?

NO

YES

JEDI

You are brave and selfless. Your duty is to defend the galaxy from evil! Stay strong – and beware the Sith.

SENATOR

You can make a difference in the galaxy. Learn to use discussion and cooperation to help your cause, and avoid greed and those who are greedy.

YES

BOUNTY HUNTER

You always look out for yourself – and will earn a good living. Just remember to be careful about who you work for.

NO

NO

SITH

You are strong, ambitious and hungry for power at any cost. But beware, the dark side will change you into something horrible.

Do you crave power more than riches?

YES

The dark side wins

  Towards the end of the Clone Wars,
Palpatine was kidnapped. Anakin and
Obi-Wan went to his aid, but it was
a trap. Sith Lord Count Dooku was
waiting for them. He knocked out
Obi-Wan and began to fight Anakin.

Palpatine urged Anakin to kill
Dooku and Anakin gave in.

A short time later Anakin chose
Palpatine over the Jedi and his
transition to the dark side was
complete. He knelt before
Palpatine – his new Sith Master.

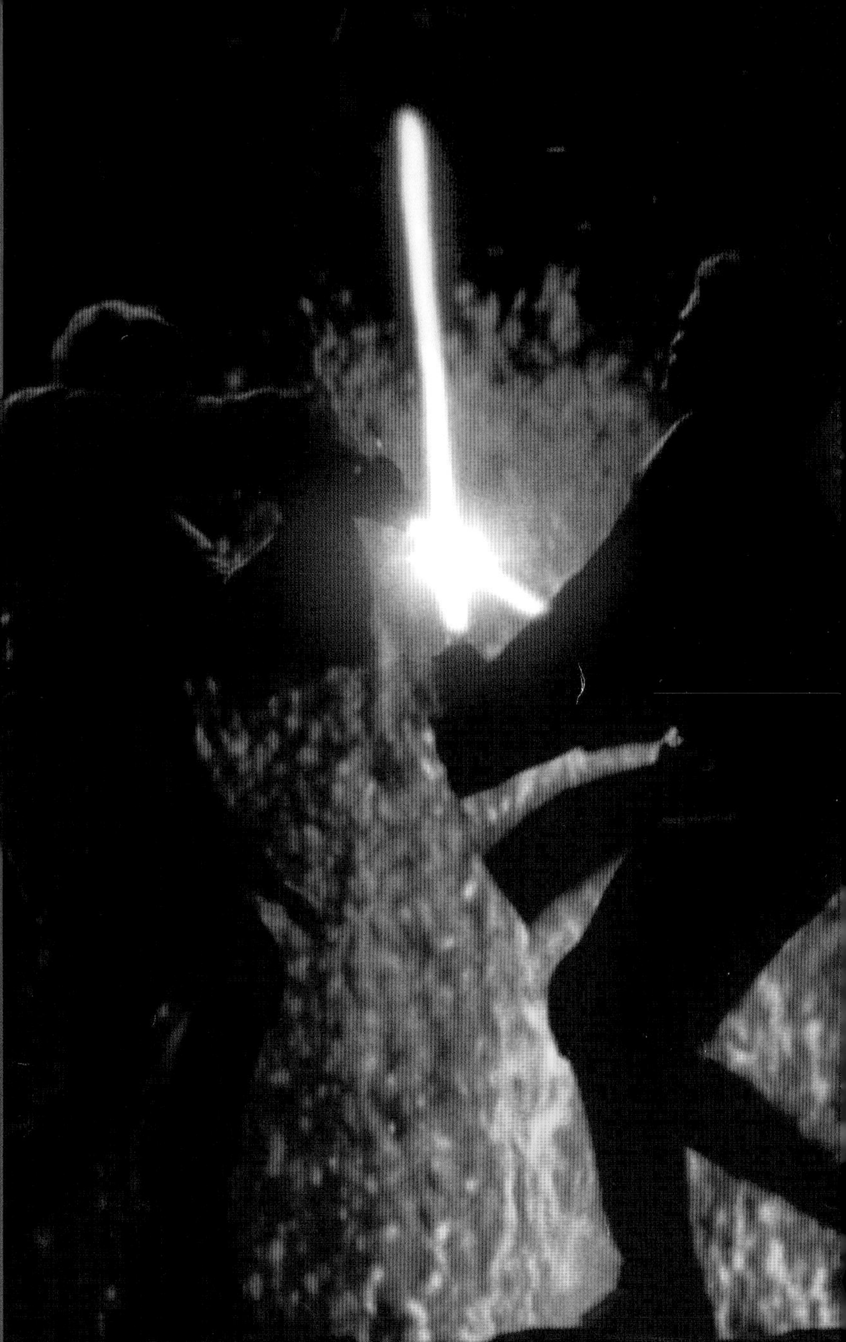

The end of Anakin

Anakin turned his back on the Jedi and adopted the Sith name Darth Vader. On Palpatine's orders he set out to destroy his former friends and comrades. Darth Vader also became convinced that Padmé and Obi-Wan were plotting against him. He nearly killed his wife and then faced Obi-Wan in an intense lightsaber battle.

Although Darth Vader was driven by anger and the power of the dark side, Obi-Wan won the terrible fight. Vader suffered horrific injuries and burns.

The creation of Darth Vader

Although Darth Vader's body seemed beyond repair, Palpatine refused to give up on his evil apprentice. He took Vader's body to a secret medical facility where it was rebuilt using cyber-technology. Vader needed special breathing equipment and life-support systems just to stay alive.

Behind the black armour and a black helmet, it seemed that no part of the human Anakin Skywalker was left. Darth Vader had given himself completely to the ways of the dark side.

BUILDING DARTH VADER

Saving the life of the new Sith apprentice was no easy task.

Medical Kit
First, Darth Sidious used special tools and medicines.

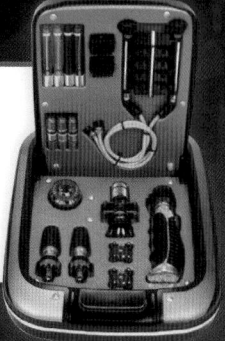

Droids
Next, the medical droids helped fix all of Darth Vader's injuries.

Reconstruction
The droids also added mechanical body parts to replace Darth Vader's limbs.

Armour

Finally, Darth Vader was covered in strong black armour to protect his body.

Helmet
Allows Vader to breathe and protects his face

Chest control box
Monitors Darth Vader's life support

Belt control panel
Regulates armour temperature

37

Padmé's secret

With her husband lost to the dark side, a heartbroken Padmé gave birth to twins, whom she named Luke and Leia. Loyal Jedi Master Obi-Wan Kenobi was by her side, but Padmé had no will to live without Anakin.

Jedi Master Yoda decided to keep the children a secret from their father. Obi-Wan took Luke to Tatooine to live with Shmi Skywalker's stepson, Owen Lars, and his wife, Beru.

Luke's life on the desert planet was hard and lonely. Leia, was taken to the planet Alderaan. She was adopted by Obi-Wan's friend Bail Organa and brought up a princess. Neither twin knew that the other existed. They did not suspect that their father was the feared Sith Lord Vader.

The rise of Darth Vader

The Republic had been destroyed and the evil Palpatine ruled the galaxy as Emperor, with Darth Vader by his side. The Sith Lords would let nothing and no one stand in their way. Vader's terrifying appearance, deep voice and loud artificial breathing struck fear into the hearts of his enemies and allies alike. Even his own generals could not escape Vader's wrath and, as time went by, the Sith's powers grew even stronger.

Anakin Skywalker had been a brave pilot and skilled with a lightsaber, but the dark side of the Force continued to corrupt Darth Vader. He strangled people using the Force and could read the thoughts of others.

Civil war

Although the Sith had destroyed the Republic and most of the Jedi, a small group of rebels bravely opposed the Empire. Known as the Rebel Alliance, they were based on the planet Yavin 4. Little did Darth Vader know that two of the rebels were his children, Luke and Leia.

The famous Jedi Master Obi-Wan Kenobi faced his former apprentice once again.

This time Obi-Wan let Darth Vader win in order to show Luke that, thanks to the Force, a person's spirit continues after death.

Rebel victory

The Emperor decided to build a superweapon known as a Death Star. It was the size of a small moon and had the power to blow up entire planets.

However, the rebels managed to obtain the plans for the weapon and learned that it had a fatal flaw. One exhaust port was unprotected and if a pilot fired torpedoes into its shaft, a chain reaction of explosions would destroy the whole Death Star. The rebels sent a squadron of star fighters and their best pilot, Luke Skywalker, had one chance to destroy the Death Star.

He did not miss.

Imperial fleet

The Rebel Alliance had only
a small number of ships which
already bore the scars of previous
battles, but the Empire had a massive
fleet of starships. The largest and most
powerful Imperial vessels
were known as Super Star
Destroyers. Powered by
13 engines, the Super Star
Destroyers were arrow
shaped and loaded with
deadly weapons.

Darth Vader's ship *Executor* was the most powerful Super Star Destroyer. Vader commanded the fleet, but the Emperor gave his orders via hologram.

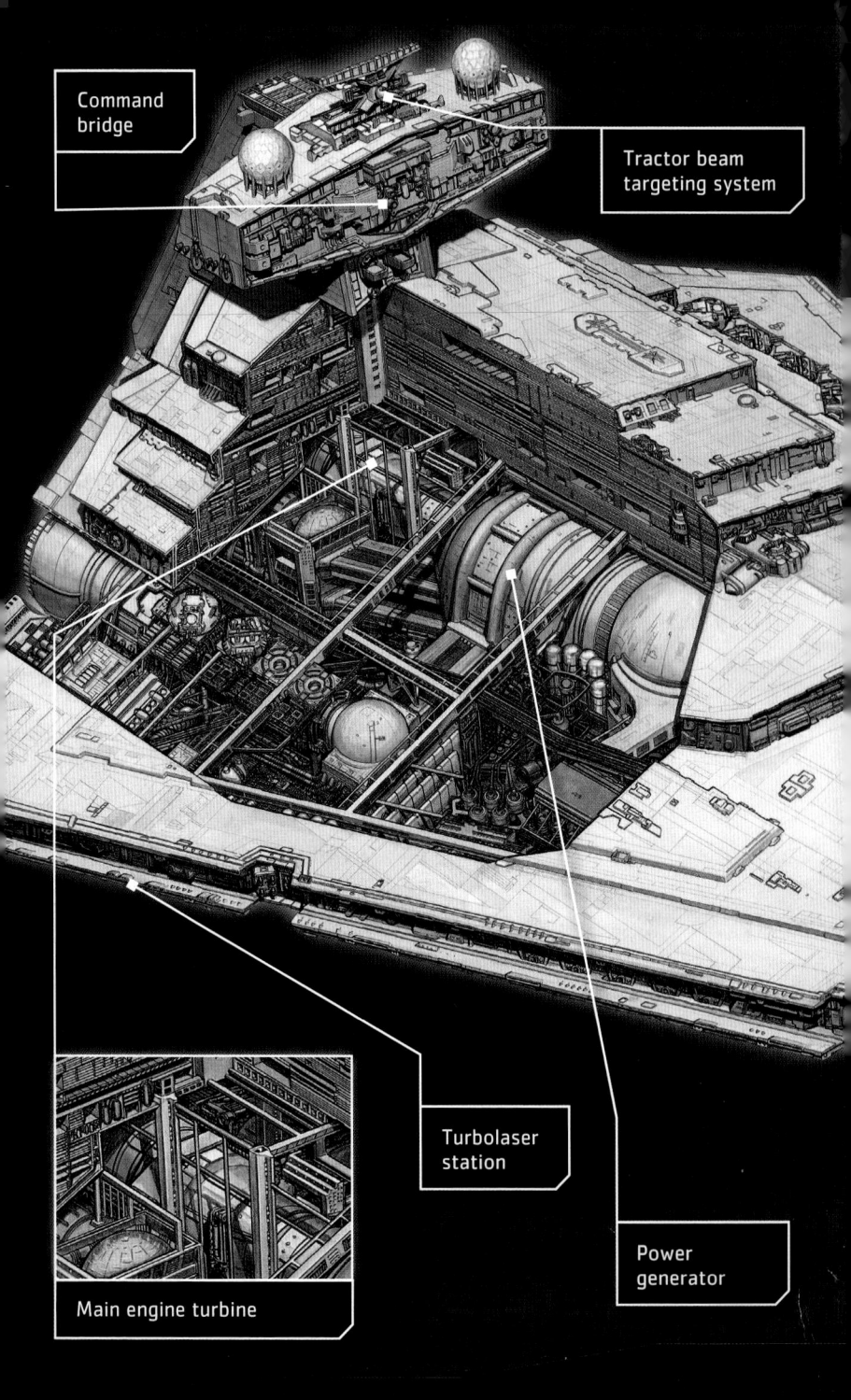

Command
bridge

Tractor beam
targeting system

Turbolaser
station

Power
generator

Main engine turbine

STAR DESTROYER

The Star Destroyer is a symbol of the Empire's military might. It carries powerful weapons and armies across the galaxy to fight those who oppose the imperial rule.

Flight deck control

Tractor beam power cells

Reactor

Main TIE landing bay

Tractor beams

49

Vader's revenge

When the rebels blew up the first Death Star, it made Darth Vader and the Emperor extremely angry. They began building a new Death Star, and Darth Vader set out to find and destroy the rebels responsible.

Vader sent probe droids to every corner of the galaxy to find the rebels' new base. He finally located them on the ice planet Hoth.

The Sith Lord travelled to Hoth with the Imperial fleet and launched a deadly attack. The rebels had to evacuate very quickly and their forces were scattered far and wide across the galaxy.

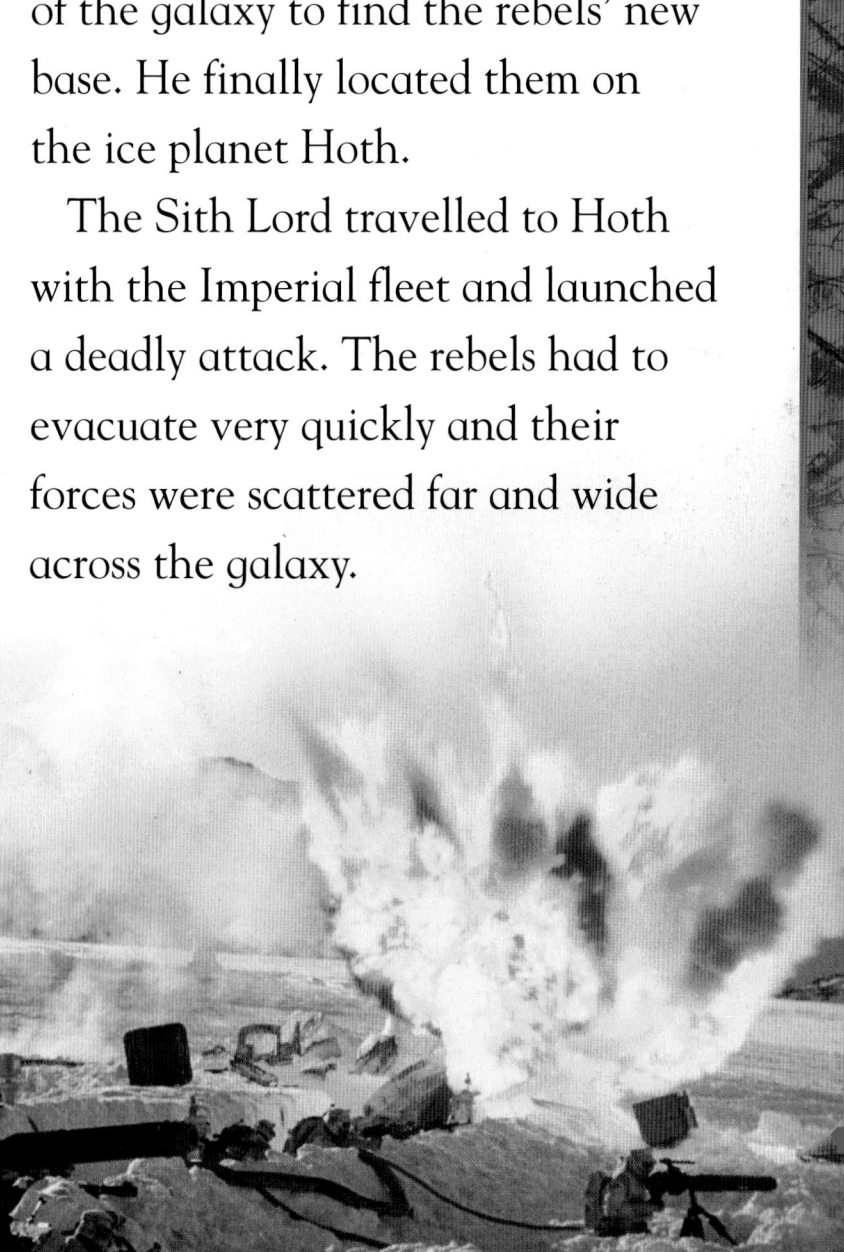

Cloud City

Emperor Palpatine had finally
told Darth Vader the truth about
Luke Skywalker. As Darth Vader
laid a trap for Luke on Cloud City,
he was looking for more than just
a troublesome rebel – he was searching
for his son.

As Luke and Vader fought with
lightsabers, Luke still had no idea
who lay behind Darth Vader's mask.
The fight ended when Vader chopped
off Luke's hand. He revealed that he
was Luke's father and asked his son
to join him and rule the galaxy.
Despite his painful wound, Luke was
strong with the Force. He refused
to turn to the dark side.

LIKE FATHER, LIKE SON

In many ways, the lives of Anakin and Luke Skywalker have followed similar paths.

LATE TO THE JEDI ORDER

Nine-year-old Anakin is a lot older than most children who begin their Jedi training.

Luke begins his Jedi training when he is 22 years old – much older than any Padawan before him.

VERY STRONG IN THE FORCE

Anakin's Force skills help him pilot his spaceship at incredible speeds.

Luke uses his Jedi reflexes to pilot his spaceship and destroy the Death Star.

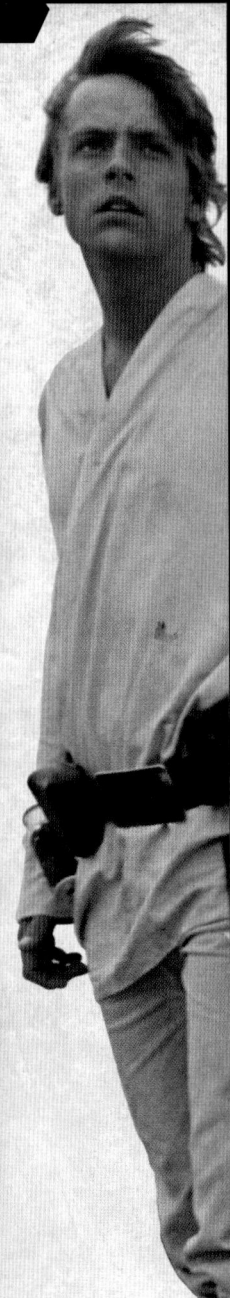

DISOBEDIENT

Anakin ignores many Jedi teachings, including the rule that a Jedi must not become overly attached to others.

Luke does not take Yoda's advice about completing his Jedi training. He runs off to help his friends.

SCARRED IN BATTLE

Anakin loses his right hand during a duel with Darth Tyranus. It reminds him of his inexperience.

Darth Vader cuts off Luke's right hand in a duel. It reminds Luke of his similarity to his father.

"I AM A JEDI, LIKE MY FATHER BEFORE ME."
Luke Skywalker

Vader's choice

For many years, Darth Vader had been loyal to Emperor Palpatine. However, meeting his son Luke – a good and true person – seemed to change him. Could it be that some part of Anakin Skywalker remained behind Vader's mask?

Palpatine had predicted that Luke would come to them and he would be turned to the dark side. When Luke surrendered, it seemed that Palpatine would be proved right. As father and son fought once more, Luke felt anger and hatred and drew close to the dark side.

At the last moment Luke was able to control his feelings and refused to join the dark side. As an enraged Palpatine attacked Luke, Anakin Skywalker finally returned from the dark side to save his son.

The death of Darth Vader

At the vital moment, Darth Vader returned from his nightmare. Luke had reminded him that he was once a great Jedi named Anakin Skywalker. However, as Vader saved his son, he was fatally wounded by the Emperor.

As Anakin lay dying, he asked Luke to remove his helmet so that he could look at his son's face with his own eyes. When Anakin died, his body disappeared into the light side of the Force. Luke was sad that his father was dead but proud of him, too. The light side of the Force had overcome the dark side and Anakin Skywalker had returned.

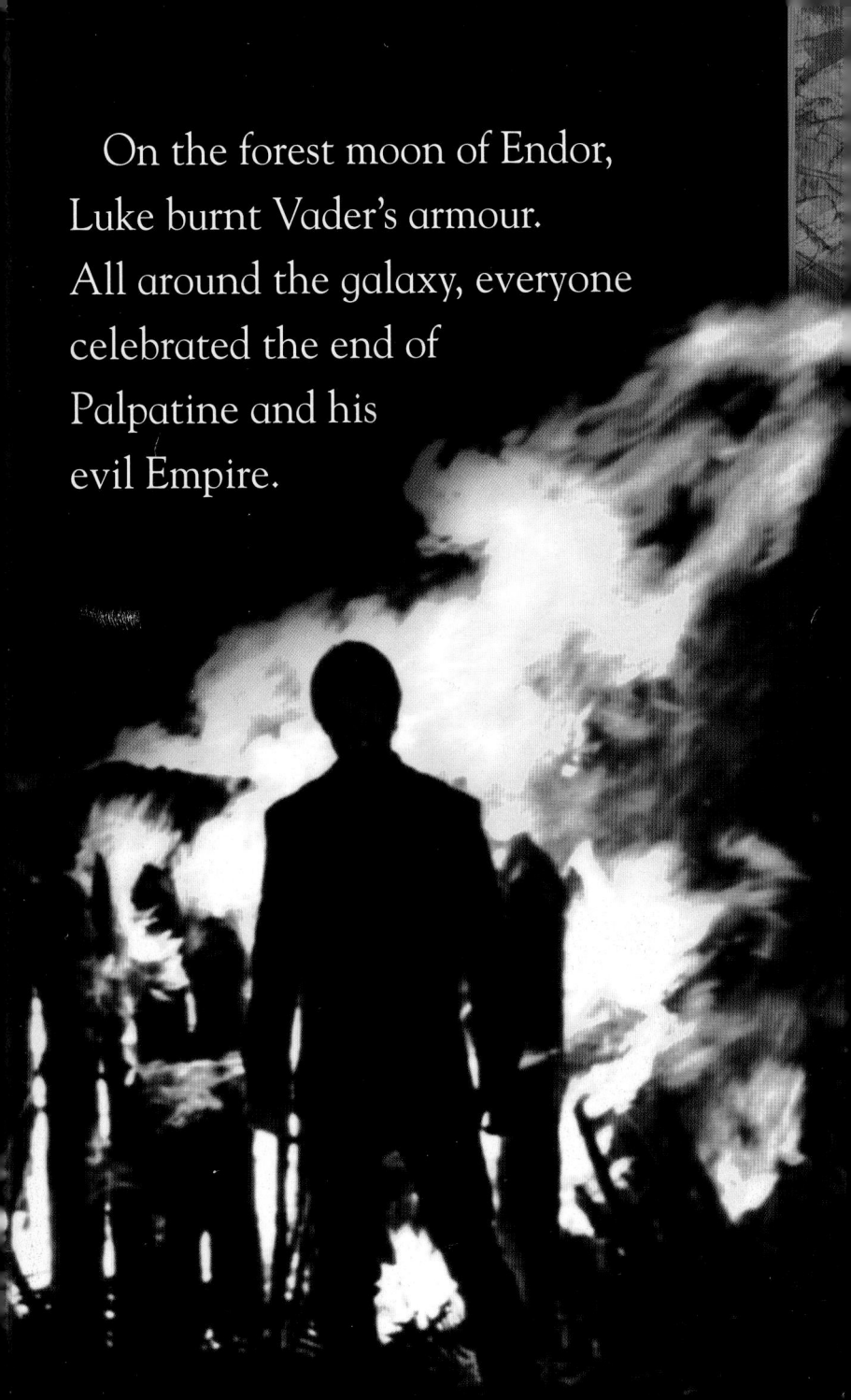

On the forest moon of Endor,
Luke burnt Vader's armour.
All around the galaxy, everyone
celebrated the end of
Palpatine and his
evil Empire.

Glossary

Grief
Very strong feeling of sadness.

Jedi Knight
A warrior with special powers who defends the galaxy from evil.

Liberated
To be free from the control of a person, group or government.

Lightsaber
A Jedi and Sith weapon, made of glowing energy.

Rebel
Someone who opposes whoever is in power.

Representatives
People chosen to act or speak for others.

Sinister
Giving a feeling that something evil or bad is happening or could happen.

Index

Guide for Parents

DK Reads is a three-level interactive reading adventure series for children, developing the habit of reading widely for both pleasure and information. These chapter books have an exciting main narrative interspersed with a range of reading genres to suit your child's reading ability, as required by the National Curriculum. Each book is designed to develop your child's reading skills, fluency, grammar awareness and comprehension in order to build confidence and engagement when reading.

Ready for a *Starting to Read Alone* book

YOUR CHILD SHOULD

- be able to read most words without needing to stop and break them down into sound parts.
- read smoothly, in phrases and with expression. By this level, your child will be mostly reading silently.
- self-correct when some word or sentence doesn't sound right.

A Valuable and Shared Reading Experience

For some children, text reading, particularly non-fiction, requires much effort but adult participation can make this both fun and easier. So here are a few tips on how to use this book with your child.

TIP 1 Check out the contents together before your child begins:

- Invite your child to check the blurb, contents page and layout of the book and comment on it.
- Ask your child to make predictions about the story.
- Chat about the information your child might want to find out.

TIP 2 Encourage fluent and flexible reading:

- Support your child to read in fluent, expressive phrases, making full use of punctuation and thinking about the meaning.
- Encourage your child to slow down and check information where appropriate.

TIP 3 Indicators that your child is reading for meaning:

- Your child will be responding to the text if he/she is self-correcting and varying his/her voice.
- Your child will want to chat about what he/she is reading or is eager to turn the page to find out what will happen next.

TIP 4 Praise, share and chat:

- The factual pages tend to be more difficult than the story pages, and are designed to be shared with your child.
- Encourage your child to recall specific details after each chapter.
- Provide opportunities for your child to pick out interesting words and discuss what they mean.
- Discuss how the author captures the reader's interest, or how effective the non-fiction layouts are.
- Ask questions about the text. These help to develop comprehension skills and awareness of the language used.

A FEW ADDITIONAL TIPS

- Read to your child regularly to demonstrate fluency, phrasing and expression; to find out or check information; and for sharing enjoyment.
- Encourage your child to reread favourite texts to increase reading confidence and fluency.
- Check that your child is reading a range of different types, such as poems, jokes and following instructions.

Have you read these other great books from DK?

STARTING TO READ ALONE

Test what makes rockets fly. Which design would you use?

Join the heroes of the rebellion as they continue to fight the Empire.

© 2015 Lucasfilm Ltd and ™

Meet the heroes of Chima™ and help them find the Legend Beasts.

© 2015 The LEGO Group

READING ALONE

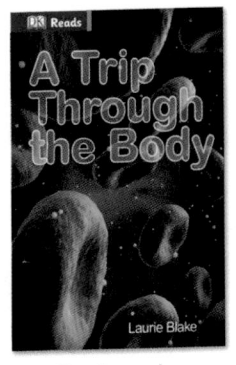

Explore the amazing systems at work inside the human body.

Join a life-or-death futuristic adventure to find a new home planet.

Read all about the scariest monsters in the Star Wars galaxy.

© 2015 Lucasfilm Ltd and ™